Original title:
The Apple Tree's Gift

Copyright © 2025 Creative Arts Management OÜ
All rights reserved.

Author: Arabella Whitmore
ISBN HARDBACK: 978-1-80586-333-5
ISBN PAPERBACK: 978-1-80586-805-7

Embrace of the Bounty

In the orchard where the laughter flows,
A plucky fruit with a shiny pose.
Wobbly branches dance and sway,
While squirrels plot to steal away.

A chubby fellow, red and round,
On my head, it makes a sound.
I tripped on grass, the fruit took flight,
Landing on the cat—oh what a sight!

The neighbors spy through garden gates,
To watch my mishaps and debates.
With pies in mind, I harvest bold,
But slippery slips make stories told.

With every bite, a squirt follows,
My shirt adorned with juicy swallows.
So here I sit, in sweet despair,
As fruit-filled fun goes everywhere!

Harvests of Autumn's Whisper

Leaves turn gold, a crisp delight,
Squirrels dance, what a funny sight!
Laughter echoes through the air,
As fruits drop down without a care.

Pumpkins roll in a game of chance,
While slimy snails perform a dance.
Cider flows in every cup,
Toasting trees, we raise it up!

Beneath the Boughs of Riches

Boughs bend low, a treasure trove,
Here comes Farmer Bob in a grove.
Basket in hand, he sings a tune,
Maybe he'll find a dancing prune!

The pears are plump, the laughter loud,
A donkey joins, he feels so proud.
With every bite, the jokes ignite,
A fruity feast, what pure delight!

Orchard Secrets Unveiled

Secrets whispered on the breeze,
Where apples giggle in the trees.
Hiding from the hungry tongue,
Pretending silence, they're still young!

The cider press is working fast,
Oh, watch those bubbles, it's a blast!
A splash of juice, a sudden slip,
Look out below! It's one big trip!

Fruits of Love in Leafy Shadows

In shadows cool, the lovers meet,
A hearty snack, a tasty treat.
A snack so red, it rolls away,
Chasing each other, what a play!

A dance of love, a playful twirl,
They find themselves in a fruity swirl.
With laughter ripe, their hearts take flight,
In leafy bounds, their joy's in sight!

Sylvan Serenade

In a grove where laughs collide,
Fruits fall down, oh what a ride!
Squirrels dance with cheeky flair,
Chasing apples through the air.

A grin on each plump little face,
Rolling fruits, an endless race.
Beneath the branches, giggles soar,
Nature's joke that we adore!

Patchwork of Fragrance

A waft of sweetness fills the breeze,
Buzzing bees on bended knees.
Lemonade spills as kids all scream,
Wishing apples would grow on cream!

Leaves whisper secrets, tales of yore,
As ants march in a tiny chore.
Underfoot, the treasures lie,
Who knew fruit could make us fly?

The Sweet Symphony

Notes of crunch with every bite,
A chorus of flavor, pure delight.
Parents chuckle at sticky hands,
Kids invent their own fruit bands!

Pies and jams, the treats abound,
Laughter echoes all around.
With every munch, our worries flee,
In this fruity jubilee!

Abundant Arms

Branches stretch, a playful reach,
Drawing near for a fruity peach.
Silly hats on heads so small,
Underneath, we're bound to sprawl!

Harvest moon and lantern light,
Kids dance silly, what a sight!
With laughter echoing through the night,
An orchard's gift, pure delight!

A Dance of Seasons

Leaves tap dance in the breeze,
While squirrels practice their tease.
Branches wave in playful cheer,
    As winter's chill gets near.

A Dance of Seasons

Fruits wear jackets, furry and bright,
Talking smack beneath the moonlight.
Bugs hold disco parties 'round,
On juicy beats, the sweetness found.

Savoring Nature's Rich Palette

Colors splashed like paint on a plate,
Bees buzzing jokes, never late.
Honey drips like laughter's flow,
As daisies gossip about the show.

Savoring Nature's Rich Palette

Giggling blooms in a flower race,
Sunshine slaps on a cheery face.
Wind whispers tales of silly sprites,
As nature serves up its delights.

The Heart of the Grove

In the grove where laughter lingers,
Fruits juggle with their tiny fingers.
Chirps and chuckles fill the air,
As critters dance without a care.

The Heart of the Grove

Roots tell secrets of the night,
While shadows break into the light.
The heart beats in joyful splendor,
Nature's ball is always tender.

Ripened Moments

Time's a ripe fruit falling slow,
With each drop, the giggles grow.
Biting into moments, sweet and bright,
Life's a salad, mixed just right.

Ripened Moments

Seeds of laughter, scattered wide,
Harvest joy, let hearts decide.
In every crunch and tasty thrill,
Ripened moments bring the chill.

Sunlit Berry Kisses

In the garden, fruits so bright,
Strawberries giggle in the light.
Ripe tomatoes, blushing red,
Whisper secrets in my head.

Bananas swing from leafy tops,
They joke about their funny hops.
Peppers dance with silly flair,
While lemons grin without a care.

Whimsy of the Orchard Path

Wobbling pears roll down the lane,
Chasing shadows, feeling vain.
Plums in pockets, what a sight,
Hopping high with sheer delight.

Cherries laugh, they form a band,
Playing tunes on wishful sand.
With every step, a jest unspools,
As apples juggle with the fools.

Echoing Laughter of the Leaves

Leaves are giggling in the breeze,
Tickling branches, oh what tease!
Squirrels chuckle, take a peek,
In this orchard, joy's unique.

Crunchy acorns join the fun,
Whirling 'round, they love to run.
Every rustle sings a rhyme,
Nature's comedy, pure sublime.

The Promise of the Coming Year

Seeds are dreaming in the ground,
Hatching jokes from underground.
Next spring's sprouts will cause a stir,
With whimsical paths, they'll confer.

Blooming laughter fills the air,
Buds preparing for their flair.
While winter snores with frosty hush,
Future fruits create a lush.

Sweet Surrender on the Branches

Beneath the sun, the apples sway,
With rosy cheeks, they laugh and play.
A squirrel scurries, nimble and spry,
Munching treats as the branches sigh.

The farmer chuckles, scratching his head,
"What a buffet! They'll soon be fed!"
He dances round in a goofy spree,
While the fruits giggle, as bright as can be.

A pie in the oven, that's the plan,
But those sneaky apples, they hatch a scam.
They roll and tumble, causing a mess,
"Thanks for the laughter! You're really the best!"

So gather round, let the fun begin,
With tart surprises, where do I begin?
Laughter and sweetness filled with delight,
This orchard's a circus, oh what a sight!

Nature's Bounty in Orchard Light

In orchard glow, the fruits conspire,
To send the farmer, high on a wire.
"We're ripe for fun!" they seem to cheer,
As he stumbles and tumbles, that's his career!

A bee buzzes in with a flirty tune,
Dancing round blossoms, a waltz with the moon.
The apples shout out, "Hey, don't forget!"
"We're here to play tricks; can you take the bet?"

A ladder nearby, but they're out of reach,
"Catch me if you can!" is the lesson they teach.
With each step he takes, they roll just a bit,
The orchard's a comedy, never to quit!

Cider in hand, he laughs with surprise,
As apples throw pranks, right before his eyes.
A harvest of chuckles, with a fruity twist,
In nature's own bounty, it's hard to resist!

Echoes of Abundant Seasons

Once upon a time, in an orchard prime,
Apples grew bold, and shook off the grime.
They whispered and giggled, with each breeze that blew,
"We've got some tricks up our sleeves for you!"

The farmer arrives with his trusted friend,
A basket that's empty, they just can't pretend.
"Let's fill it up!" he calls with delight,
But the apples just chuckle and giggle in flight.

A pie is the goal, or so he believes,
Yet apples roll around, waving their leaves.
"Catch us if you can!" they shout with delight,
As he dives and he ducks, what a comical sight!

With barrels of laughter, the harvest was grand,
But pies were a dream, unmade and unplanned.
Still, with heart full of joy and a grin ear to ear,
The funny fruit feast was what brought him cheer!

Gifts of Perseverance and Patience

In the garden of dreams, the apples do thrive,
With whispers of mischief, they come alive.
"Patience is key!" seems their playful call,
Yet they bounce 'round like they're having a ball.

A neighbor comes by, with a curious glance,
"What's happening here? Are they starting a dance?"
The fruits laugh and chuckle, then plop on the ground,
Creating a tumble—a joyous sound!

Trying to harvest? It's a game on repeat,
Each time he gets close, they scurry on feet.
"We're ripe for the picking, but not just yet!"
His basket is empty; this is quite the duet!

With good humor shared, like a sweet little jest,
The fruits finally yield, all so happy, and blessed.
For laughter it seems is the ultimate prize,
In the orchard of patience, under bright sunny skies!

Orchard Reverie

In the orchard, fruit does tease,
Bouncing apples in the breeze,
Squirrels scurry, eyes so wide,
Stealing snacks, they cannot hide.

With a plop, down they fall,
Beneath the trees, let's have a ball,
Juicy bites and laughter ring,
Nature's joy, she loves to sing.

Every fruit a sweet delight,
Worms with hats, oh what a sight!
Ants will march in endless line,
Carrying crumbs, how they dine!

So let's dance beneath the shade,
In this fruity, fun brigade,
Laughter echoes, day well spent,
This orchard, we shall not repent.

Cascade of Colors

A splash of red, a dash of green,
Dancing apples, what a scene!
In a bucket, they all roll,
A game of catch with fruity soul.

Giggling girls and boys in tow,
Who can catch the biggest show?
Each triumphant apple snatch,
Ends in laughter, quite a match!

Colors burst, a painter's dream,
Caught up in an autumn stream,
With every bite, a silly noise,
Who knew fruit could bring such joys?

When the juice drips down the chin,
Grins can't help, they spill within,
A colorful cascade it seems,
In our orchard, we weave our dreams.

Echoes of the Generous Past

Once an orchard, oh so grand,
Now it's stuffed with pies so planned,
Baking dreams, the oven hums,
Aye, from fruit, the laughter comes!

Grandma's recipe, a top secret,
Spills in jars, oh what a treat!
Dancing spoons and floured faces,
Laughter fills nostalgic spaces.

Beneath the tree, bashful bees,
Buzzing rounds with charming ease,
Can you hear that merry buzz?
Every pie made just because!

Echoes of the past still play,
In our hearts, they twist and sway,
With every crumb shared by friends,
We know the joy, it never ends.

Fields of Giving

In the field we play all day,
Chasing fruit in a playful way,
Rolling pumpkins, apples too,
All around, the laughter grew!

Cider flows like water streams,
Rich and sweet, we create dreams,
Sip by sip, but oh what fun,
Each giggle makes the glasses run!

The harvest dance, we twirl and sway,
With every bite, we laugh and play,
Friends come in from near and far,
Here in fields, we are the stars!

So gather round, let's share the cheer,
Nature's bounty, all right here,
With fruity gifts, our hearts so bold,
In fields of giving, joy takes hold.

Journey to the Core

Once I climbed to grab a treat,
This fruit was stuck, oh what a feat!
I slipped and tumbled, hit the ground,
My dreams of pie, all scattered around.

Branches waving with a grin,
Hopeful fruit, oh where to begin?
A saucer waits, a craving grows,
Yet here I am, in apple prose.

The peel's a slippery, tricky foe,
Did I get the snack? I don't think so!
A worm peeks out and calls me friend,
I guess this journey has no end.

So as I laugh, I take a seat,
Enjoy my time, the sun's so sweet.
With every bite, I'll take my chance,
In this game of fruit, I'll always dance!

Shadows of Abundant Grace

Underneath the leafy throne,
I found a treasure, all my own.
An apple's shape, oh how it shines,
But it rolled away—thank you, vines!

It sparked a chase, so full of glee,
Fell flat on dirt, oh woe is me!
A munchkin's dream, a taste divine,
But getting it back, now that's the line.

I slipped, I slid, danced like a fool,
To catch that fruit, a fishing pool.
You think it's sweet? I think it's sly,
This crafty snack that loves to fly!

Now here I sit, a pie in mind,
With apples gone, I'm in a bind.
Yet laughter bubbles, fills the space,
In shadows of that juicy grace!

Whispers in the Wind

They say the apples sing in trees,
But as I listen, oh, what tease!
They giggle, chuckle in the breeze,
While I just stand, lost in the leaves.

A whimsy thought, a curious mind,
What fun awaits, oh fruit, so blind!
I'll make a pie, or so I claim,
But all I taste is sour shame.

A chat with worms, a secret keep,
"To us it's fun, to you, just sleep!"
But here I am, a giggle fits,
For every bite, there's endless flits.

So let them whisper, let them talk,
A dance with nature, let it rock.
With laughter floating, heart so free,
I'll find my joy in this apple spree!

Reflections of Golden Days

Golden fruit hanging from the bough,
I reach up high, with furrowed brow.
But slippery skin, oh what a tease,
I'm on a quest, down on my knees.

With one big tug, the branch did sway,
I lost my balance, oh what a display!
Down I tumbled with a splashy cheer,
Would someone pass me a mug of beer?

I laugh, I cry, with fruit in hair,
The squirrels just giggle, if they dare.
The bees hum songs, they join the fun,
All the while, I chow down, yum!

As golden days pass with a wink,
I'll chase these apples, and share a drink.
For in this orchard, fun comes my way,
With laughter ringing, brightening the day!

Beneath the Canopy of Generosity

In the shade where laughter grows,
Squirrels giggle, striking poses.
A friendly robin waddles near,
Stealing snacks, oh dear, oh dear!

Every branch a joker's stage,
With antics that can't be outraged.
The fruits may fall, but who can tell?
The ground's a cushion, oh what a spell!

With every crunch, a drippy smile,
Sticky fingers, crazy style.
Underneath the leafy boughs,
We laugh out loud, we make vows!

Share the bounty, hear the cheer,
Every laugh, a slice of pear.
Life's a party in this place,
Where silly meets the soft embrace.

Roots Deep, Dreams High

Roots like jokes twist underground,
Whispers of mischief all around.
One foot slips, a tumble's fate,
We laugh so hard, we can't debate!

Beneath the ground, they wiggle tight,
While up above, dreams take flight.
A bee buzzes with jokes to share,
Makes the flowers dance and flare!

Twirling in a silly sway,
Dreams grow tall, in bright array.
With every giggle, hope does sprout,
In this merry little bout!

When the sunset paints the sky,
We gather 'round, and we won't lie.
These roots of jest, they intertwine,
In every laugh, we feel divine.

The Whispering Leaves of Legacy

Leaves that chuckle, rustle wide,
Sharing secrets, a playful ride.
A breeze pulls 'em, whispering fun,
Tales of mischief, second to none!

Each flutter tells a joke or two,
Making clouds giggle, oh so blue.
From little seeds, great tales arise,
Sprouting laughs beneath sunny skies!

Beneath the colors, silly reflects,
A legacy of laughter connects.
As branches sway, our hearts align,
With every breeze, a punchline!

We gather 'round the stories told,
Of lovesick bees and thieves so bold.
In every leaf a memory's spun,
Life's a comedy, oh what fun!

Tapestry of Fruitful Yields

A patchwork quilt of fruity cheer,
Strawberries whisper, 'Come over here!'
Mangoes giggle, sweet and bright,
In this tapestry, pure delight!

Bananas peel in silly ways,
Making faces for all our days.
Orange slices tell us jokes,
While playful pears dance like folks!

In every bite, a tale unfolds,
Laughter bursts, as joy beholds.
Underneath the colorful spread,
Who knew fruit could jive and tread?

Our feast of giggles, share and share,
With sunny smiles and loving care.
Together we weave this joyful tune,
In the orchard's laughter, we'll swoon!

Treasures Found in Unexpected Places

Once I tripped on a yellow fruit,
It rolled away, so resolute.
Chased it down, what a sight,
Turns out it's a snack, pure delight!

Beneath a branch, I found a shoe,
Best left alone, I just knew.
But next to it, a sandwich lay,
Guess I'll dine here today!

A squirrel chuckled, made me smile,
He knew my plans all the while.
I munched on gems from nature's stock,
While laughing at my own clock!

Therefore I'll wander, trunk and root,
Searching for treasures, oh what a hoot!
Life's little quirks can surely please,
With hidden finds beneath the trees!

Dreams Served on a Silver Platter

Last night I dreamed of juicy pies,
Dancing elephants and flying fries.
When I awoke, what did I see?
A shiny platter just for me!

It had a note, though poorly scrawled,
'Treat yourself, you're enthralled!'
I found some apples, shiny and round,
The platter sang, oh what a sound!

My friends all gasped, thought I'd gone mad,
Where's the cake? They looked so sad.
But when we bit, we couldn't jest,
These apples were, simply the best!

So dreams on platters can be fun,
Delicious treats from dawn till sun.
In wacky dreams, we may connect,
With laughter, joy, and sweet respect!

Timeless Cycles of Giving

An old tree stood, with roots so deep,
It whispered secrets, made us leap.
'Take a bite, share a grin,
Fruits of joy, let laughter spin!'

With every season, fruits would fall,
A funny dance, a merry brawl.
Kids ran wide, and squealed so bright,
With each pluck, we felt delight.

"Oh no!" cried Max, "I slipped on goo!"
As apples rained, like morning dew.
We giggled hard, then gathered round,
In messy games, true fun we found!

So here's to cycles, buy a round,
In every bite, true joy is found.
Embrace the laughter, let love flow,
In every season, let it grow!

Nature's Caress in Every Bite

One sunny day, beneath the sun,
An apple said, 'Come have some fun!'
With a grin, I took a tug,
Squeezed it tight like a friendly hug.

The juice shot out, right in my face,
I laughed so hard, a silly race!
Nature's gifts can spark a cheer,
When food fights happen, we persevere!

A bite of tart, a taste so sweet,
With every crunch, our hearts do beat.
We swirl around, we dance and prance,
A fruity fiesta, what a chance!

So join the feast, and don't be shy,
Curly worms might wave goodbye.
In every bite, the fun ignites,
Nature's laughter in our sights!

Embracing Autumn's Rich Palette

The leaves are falling like pizza slices,
Dancing in air with wild surprises.
Squirrels wearing hats, oh what a sight,
Gathering treasures with all their might.

Pumpkins rolling down the lane,
Playing tag, oh what a game!
The breeze is chuckling, or is it me?
Who knew autumn could be so free?

Cider flows like rivers of cheer,
While acorns clink like pints of beer.
Mushrooms sprout like umbrella hats,
Singing tunes with wandering rats.

The harvest moon has too much fun,
Painting the world, oh what a stun.
Join the dance, let laughter ring,
In this season, we're all the kings!

A Dance of Colors Against the Sky.

The sun sets like a pie that's baked,
Colors swirling, oh what fun we've raked!
Purple, yellow, red, and brown,
Like a clown's best suit in a joyful town.

Clouds are cotton candy treats,
Drifting above like lazy beats.
The wind's giggles bring a cheer,
As we stomp our feet like a new frontier.

Riding leaves on a swirling gust,
Jumping in puddles, humor's a must.
Scarecrows laughing, whole fields awake,
Playing tricks, oh what a prank to make!

So let us paint the skies so bright,
With giggles and grins that feel just right.
A canvas of laughter, wide and free,
Autumn's magic, just you and me!

Whispers of the Orchard

In the orchard, what a mess!
Fruit on the ground, oh, nothing less.
A worm in the apple, quite the surprise,
Doing the tango, what a disguise!

Birds are chattering tales of old,
Of apples that danced and turned to gold.
Squirrels gossip, tails all a-twitch,
Plotting their pranks, oh what a rich niche!

Under the branches, we hear a jest,
Bunch of bees buzzing, they're quite the pest.
Pollinating jokes, they say it's a blast,
Creating honey that's made to last.

Grab a basket, let's go for a ride,
With laughter and fun, it's a joyride!
In the orchard, every turn's a treat,
Where whispers of humor and fruits meet!

Bounty Beneath the Boughs

Under boughs where shadows play,
A treasure trove for us today.
Badger's rummaging, oh what a fuss,
Finding goodies without a bus!

The ground is sprinkled with colored bits,
As nature rhymes with silly fits.
Pumpkins are rolling, oh what a chase,
While raccoons laugh, like they own the place.

A basket's filled with juicy finds,
While bats practice their night-time binds.
Each fruit a joke, oh what a show,
Fruits with faces saying hello!

So grab a smile and join the feast,
Where every bite's a giggly beast.
In the bounty, let's taste some glee,
Beneath the boughs, just you and me!

Echoes of the Fruitful Glade

In a glade with fruits so bright,
A squirrel danced, what a sight!
It stole a pie from a picnicker,
And ran off fast, a true quick flicker.

The berries burst with juicy cheer,
As butterflies danced, oh so near!
But bees were buzzing, quite annoyed,
Demanding honey, they felt overjoyed!

A rabbit hopped, with mouth agape,
He stole a peach, his favorite shape!
Caught in the act, he froze in place,
Then dashed away with funny grace!

Under the loom of branches wide,
Laughter echoed, hearts filled with pride!
For in this glade of playful sways,
Nature's humor brightened our days!

Nature's Hidden Treasures

A hidden treasure, what a find,
A fruit that chuckles, one of a kind!
It giggles softly in the sun,
A cheeky treat, oh what fun!

The worms wore hats, so dapper and nice,
Debating who'd take the biggest slice!
While ants marched in their little parade,
Shouting 'freedom' in a fruit crusade!

A crabapple snickered, green and round,
With a wobbly dance, it spun around!
Lost its balance, fell to the ground,
All its friends roared laughter profound!

Underneath the giggling trees,
The whispers of joy ride each breeze!
For in this place of wacky delight,
Nature's treasures shine ever bright!

Beauty in Abundance

A picnic setup, looks divine,
Until a raccoon found the wine!
He twirled with glee, then fell in gropes,
We laughed so hard, we nearly choked!

Plums wore glasses, quite the flair,
Thought they could read, in the fresh air!
But every book was way too dry,
They closed their eyes and let out a sigh!

Grapes played tag, quite a mess,
Racing each other with such finesse!
Yet all fell down, in a clumsy heap,
Each burst of laughter, a memory to keep!

A feast of whimsy, fruits and cheer,
Nature's bounty brings us near!
So raise a glass to fun and play,
Beauty in abundance, lets us sway!

Orchard Dreams

In the orchard where dreams take flight,
A parrot claims the fruit's spotlight!
With jokes and puns, he stole the show,
Leaving us giggling, in overflow!

Cider bubbles burst with delight,
As children play till dusk's twilight!
Each splash of juice, a silly game,
As sticky fingers call each name!

Peaches plopped, oh what a scene,
Like cannonballs, they burst, so keen!
A fruit fight started with glee and cheer,
Laughter echoed, ringing clear!

In dreams of orchard, 'neath the trees,
Where every moment feels like a breeze!
With humorous tales of fun we glean,
Let's cherish this place, our laughter seen!

Nature's Handcrafted Gems

In the orchard where the fruit hangs low,
Bobbing squirrels dance, putting on a show.
With acorn hats, they strut with flair,
While birds whistle tunes, floating through the air.

Ripe fruit drops down, a plump juicy thud,
Splatting on the ground with a funny, sweet crud.
The critters all gather, it's quite the parade,
Over pits and seeds, their antics displayed.

The sun shines bright, casting shadows that play,
As nature's clowns frolic in a bright ballet.
A wee mouse slips over a very ripe pear,
And giggles erupt from the bugs on a dare.

With every bite taken, the joy does abound,
While bees buzz around, spinning laughter around.
We'll toast to the chaos, the fun and the zest,
Nature's gems make every moment the best!

Treasures on the Wind

Fluffy clouds drift by, like sailors at sea,
Blowing wishes along, as silly as can be.
A gust sends a tumbling, unclaimed juicy prize,
Slipping on the grass, oh what a surprise!

Chubby kids giggle, with hats all askew,
Chasing glossy orbs that glisten and goo.
One lands on a beagle, quite confused at the sight,
He sniffs, then he barks, as if that's his right.

Windy days bring treasures that taunt and tease,
Rolling through the fields, dancing with ease.
With a pop and a splash, it's a fruit's kind of game,
Even the clouds seem to shout with glee, "A fame!"

So let's crack open laughter, as sweet drops arise,
Gifts from the breezes, oh what a surprise!
Nature whispers secrets that tickle our dreams,
In the carnival of fruits, nothing's as it seems!

Beneath the Ripening Sky

Beneath the vast blue where giggles take flight,
Fruit hangs like ornaments, a colorful sight.
A raccoon in a hat gives a wink and a grin,
While squirrels in shorts plan a hasty spin.

The clouds giggle softly, puffed with delight,
As berries fall down, it's a hilarious sight.
One lands on a frog, who leaps with a croak,
While bopping his buddies, outside their green cloak.

Picking a peach becomes quite the sport,
With birds throwing apples, as if they report.
Kids running in circles, slipping with glee,
While bees join the fun, sting-free as can be.

The sun chuckles low, casting shadows so long,
As laughter erupts in nature's sweet song.
With every fruit tumble, joy fills the day,
Under a sky ripened with funny display!

The Nature of Nourishment

In the garden of munchies, where chuckles grow loud,
Grapes roll down hills, they laugh at the crowd.
Carrots in top hats prance on their toes,
While lettuces giggle, hiding beneath rows.

Each veggie a jester in sunlight's warm glow,
With peas in a pod that put on a show.
Tomatoes send splashes like tiny red throws,
While pumpkin provides punchlines, anything goes!

The fruits and the greens, they gather with cheer,
Holding a banquet, a feast full of queer.
With laughter as seasoning, joy in each bite,
Eating nature's bounty feels oh-so-right!

So let's dig in deeply, explore every dish,
For wisdom is sown in each juicy wish.
Embracing our meals with a smile and a wink,
The nature of nourishment makes us rethink!

Whimsy Among the Leaves

In the garden, a sneak peek,
A squirrel whispers, "Don't be meek!"
With a wiggle and a twist of fate,
He claims the fruit, oh, isn't it great?

A bird laughs high, on a branch so round,
"That cheeky squirrel, he's quite renowned!"
The ground below, a rumbling sound,
As treasures drop, oh what a mound!

A child skips in, with dreams of pie,
Finding critters who wave goodbye.
With sticky hands and apple goo,
They join the fun, that silly crew.

The sun sets low, with a giggle bright,
Under leaves, they dance in twilight.
All around, nature's playful show,
In the orchard, laughter's sure to grow!

Sweet Secrets Untold

Hiding sweets in a leafy nook,
The rabbit peeks, just like a book.
"Here lies treasure!" he squeaks with glee,
As ants march in, a buzzing spree.

A raccoon's mask, sneaky and sly,
"Bet you can't catch me, oh my, oh my!"
With candy jewels dropped everywhere,
The dance of chaos is in the air.

A gust of wind, a whoosh so loud,
Scaring critters, oh how they've cowed!
But laughter bubbles like springtime streams,
As they chase sparkles, lost in dreams.

When day fades out, a feast of fun,
They munch and crunch till the day is done.
Sharing sweets, a friendship gold,
In their hearts, sweet secrets unfold!

Magenta Mornings

Morning blooms in colors bright,
With giggles sparkled in warm sunlight.
A plump fruit wiggles, ready to tease,
"I'm the king! You'll bow, if you please!"

A family of birds, ready to chirp,
Flapping and flapping, a goofy troupe.
One leaps high, then falls with a thud,
"Oops! I'm stuck! Call for the bud!"

A worm peeks out, his head so small,
"Watch out, watch out, I'll start a brawl!"
He wriggles forth with a wobbly dance,
"Look at my moves! Who'll give me a chance?"

As day lightens, laughter weaves,
Bright and cheery, among the leaves.
In the orchard, silly things shine,
Sweet magenta mornings, oh so fine!

Fables of the Canopy

Legend tells of a fruity spree,
Where giggling ghosts sip apple tea.
"If you tickle me, I'll turn so bright!"
Just watch your fingers, hold on tight!

An owl perched, wise and bold,
"Listen close, to tales of old!"
With every hoot, a story spins,
Of feasts and fights, and wins and fins.

A raccoon rolls in, what a sight!
"I'm the bravest, day or night!"
But slips and tumbles make him meek,
"Let's start again, that's my technique!"

Underneath the boughs, with zest we find,
Laughter echoes, heart and mind.
Fables drift on the lively breeze,
In the canopy, adventure's keys!

Guardian of the Orchard

In the orchard, where laughter blooms,
Fruits fall down like silly balloons.
A squirrel giggles, chasing bees,
While old Mr. Smith sings with the trees.

The apples wear hats made of leaves,
While the birds dance, and the sun weaves.
Rabbits hop in a jolly race,
Each clutching snacks in a furry embrace.

The wind whispers secrets so sly,
As peaches flirt with the cloudy sky.
The pumpkins do a jig, oh so bright,
Under the moon's enchanted light.

So here's to the bounty, wild and sweet,
As critters gather for the feast, what a treat!
In this garden, where chuckles collide,
Nature's jesters, forever they'll ride.

A Tapestry of Flavors

Colors in baskets, oh what a sight,
Juicy, bold bursts, a true delight.
With giggles of grapes and cherries that pout,
Even the lemons can't help but shout.

Peaches giggle, they think they're the best,
While apples boast, 'We're sweeter than the rest!'
The farmer just chuckles, scratching his head,
Wondering which fruit will end up in bread.

Plums wear their purple like crowns up high,
While bananas slip by with a playful sigh.
Every bite's magic, a party of fun,
Bringing joy to the fields, oh what a run!

So gather your friends, let the laughter soar,
In this fruity fiesta, who could ask for more?
With nature as the chef, creating a scene,
It's truly a feast, vibrant and green.

Woven in Green

Beneath the leaves, a prankster's hide,
Lizards leap out with a joyful glide.
Grasshoppers giggle in their little bands,
As the prickly pears wave their spiny hands.

The cucumbers wear shades, trying to look cool,
While tomatoes toss seeds like in a pool.
Beans climb up poles, looking for fame,
In this garden drama, it's all a game.

A crow cracks jokes from an old oak tree,
While butterflies flutter, feeling so free.
The sun winks down, casting playful rays,
As vegetables cheer for their quirky ways.

So let's tip our hats to this silly scene,
Where nature's antics reign, bright and keen!
In laughter and colors, life's meant to be,
A tapestry woven, a sight to see.

Secrets of the Swaying Trunks

In the orchard, oh what a sight,
The trees sway gently, whispering light.
Their roots gossip tales, never shy,
While branches dance and the leaves all fly.

Beneath the boughs, a raccoon peeks,
Nibbling on treasures while the tree trunk speaks.
The winds carry laughter, a soft, playful tease,
As acorns are tossing just like the leaves.

Each tree has a secret, a story to tell,
Of apples that giggle and peaches that yell.
The branches sway rhythmically in delight,
While critters below hasten to take flight.

So join in the fun, hear nature's refrain,
Where the world is a stage, and joy holds the reign.
In this lively enclave, let your heart sing,
For in these green treasures, happiness springs.

Canvas of the Orchard

In the orchard where silliness grows,
Fruits wear shoes, and the laughter flows.
A watermelon danced on its round belly,
While the pears played tunes on a leafy jelly.

A ladybug strummed on a tiny guitar,
While a crow cawed jokes from the trunk of a car.
Bananas in tutus took turns on a swing,
As the squirrels laughed, oh, what a wild fling!

The cherries threw parties, so bright and so sweet,
With grapes in the corner doing the funky beat.
Lemons wore hats, looking quite debonair,
While apples just giggled, without a single care.

Each fruit added color to a vibrant scene,
With laughter that echoed like a silly routine.
In this orchard of mirth where the silly thrived,
Nature's own canvas where joy is derived.

Seasons of Enchantment

Springtime stumbles, a dance of delight,
Bunnies wear glasses, quite a silly sight.
Daffodils giggle, the tulips chuckle,
As rainbows slide down with a splash and a shuffle.

Summer arrives with a bright, goofy cheer,
Mangoes are sunbathing, loud and clear.
Watermelons play frisbee under the sun,
While popsicles parade, oh what funny fun!

Autumn wobbles in with leaves all a-flaunt,
Pumpkins wear sneakers, they're ready to jaunt.
Nutrias in sweaters spin tales of the breeze,
While acorns hold contests of who can tease.

Winter won't miss the whimsical show,
Where oranges wear mittens, stealing the glow.
Snowflakes are giggling, a frosty ballet,
In seasons of laughter that brighten the day.

Treetop Tales

Up in the treetops, where mischief abounds,
Squirrels tell stories, and laughter resounds.
Raccoons in tuxedos, so dapper and neat,
Invite all the critters for a grand tree meet.

High on the branches, the owls wink with glee,
As the parakeets gossip with humor so free.
A woodpecker knocks with a rhythm so keen,
While chipmunks spin tales fit for a queen.

Caterpillars debate 'bout their future flight,
While ladybugs giggle beneath twinkling light.
The air filled with chuckles and whimsical plans,
As the leaves join the dance in spontaneous fans.

Oh, treetop gatherings are always a blast,
With laughter and fun that's both silly and fast.
In the canopy's laughter, there's magic to find,
Stories of giggles that tickle the mind.

Nectar's Caress

Bumblebees buzzing with a laugh in their hum,
Flit by the blossoms where sweetness doth come.
With nectar so rich, they dance from each bud,
While butterflies joke about landing in mud.

Dew drops are diamonds on petals they play,
As bees share their tales in a jolly ballet.
The blossoms all chuckle at each honeyed note,
While a cheeky ladybug takes center wrote.

The sun says 'hello' with a wink and a ray,
As the flowers all rustle in a whimsical way.
Together they sing in a chorus divine,
In a garden of joy where the funny things shine.

So sip on the nectar, let laughter take wing,
In this bloom of delight, every heart has a swing.
With petals unfolding in a vibrant embrace,
Life blossoms in humor, the sweetest of grace.

Harvest Moon Serenade

Under the moon, we dance with flair,
Silly shadows prancing everywhere.
Laughter spills from every cheek,
As apples drop with a comical squeak.

Fruits wobble like they own the night,
Chasing us in jovial flight.
We dodge and weave with playful glee,
Harvesting giggles beneath the tree.

The moon chuckles at our silly plight,
While we feast on snacks of pure delight.
With every bite, a silly grin,
Oh, harvest time, let the fun begin!

So raise your cider, toast the fun,
As wobbly apples roll and run.
This merry dance, a sweet refrain,
Beneath the moon, we'll entertain!

An Offering of Red

Once upon a tree so red,
Where apples bounced just like they said.
In a game of catch, we took our chance,
As they flew by in a playful dance.

With laughter ringing in the air,
We picked them up without a care.
They tumbled down with giggles bright,
As we threw them back in a fruit-filled fight.

A pie was born from this funny spree,
With flaky crust, oh sweet jubilee!
But as we baked, chaos ensued,
The apples rolled with an attitude!

So here's to fruits that love to play,
In a funny, apple blaze today.
May every bite bring smiles anew,
In our kitchen of laughter, just me and you!

Roots of Memory

In the garden where good times grow,
An apple fell with a hearty glow.
It landed right atop my shoe,
And rolled away, how rude, so true!

Chasing memories from days of yore,
As I trip over roots that I once swore,
Held tales of summer, laughter, and fun,
But now they giggle as I stumble and run.

With each step, a memory pops,
Of laughter, cider, and flip-flop flops.
Nature's joke within each tree,
A treasure trove of comical glee.

So here's to roots that tickle our feet,
In a dance of nostalgia, oh so sweet!
Laughing with each wobbly yelp,
In this garden of memories, we find ourselves.

The Generous Canopy

Beneath a canopy, so vast and wide,
We gather round where laughter's our guide.
Apples rained down, in a playful show,
As we dodged the fruit with a comical flow.

The branches waved in a windy spree,
Inviting us all for a funny jubilee.
We tried to catch them, oh what a sight,
As apples taunted with all their might!

Baskets tipped, and giggles soared,
As we envisioned the pie we adored.
But each pie slice, a bouncy surprise,
Made us all laugh till we closed our eyes.

So here's to the tree, kind and bright,
Bringing fun in the soft moonlight.
Under the canopy, we'll play for days,
In an orchard of laughter, forever amaze!

Orchard's Embrace and Tender Blessings

In a patch of sky and grassy sheen,
A tree stands tall, it's quite the scene.
With fruits so red, they laugh and sway,
Whispering secrets, come out and play!

The squirrels have parties, oh what a sight,
In the branches above, from morning till night.
The apples scheme with a giggle and grin,
To roll off the branches—let the fun begin!

Underneath the shade, a picnic awaits,
With sandwiches, laughter, and fluttering plates.
The juiciest bites, not a moment to waste,
As we munch on the fruit of our orchard's taste!

But wait, oh dear, what's that in the bloom?
A cheeky little bird is making a zoom!
He steals an apple, then darts with a shout,
"Catch me if you can! There's fun all about!"

A Symphony of Ripeness

In the garden's heart where the jesters play,
Fruits of laughter dance in the sun's warm ray.
A symphony sweet, with each bite we sing,
As the branches bow low, they join in the fling!

The bees are buzzing, a lively band,
With pollen in hand, they take a grand stand.
They waltz on petals, their tiny ballet,
While we sip on cider, all worries away!

With the wind as the maestro, we cheer and clap,
Every apple's a note in this fruity flap.
The pranks and the puns, they layer the sound,
In this orchard of joy, pure merriment found!

Then a rogue apple tumbles, hitting a toe,
We all burst in laughter, oh what a show!
With giggles and grins, we share in the quest,
Of the harvest that brings out our merriest best!

From Blossom to Bounty

From buds that arrive with a whimsical flair,
To plump, juicy dreams hanging high in the air.
Each blossom a promise of laughter to come,
As we chase after butterflies having some fun!

The sun draws them close, each ripened delight,
Twisting and turning, they hang on so tight.
With every soft rustle, the giggles ignite,
As apples roll down, a spectacular sight!

With baskets in hand, we gather—oh my!
The apples declare, "Let's give it a try!"
As we toss and we catch, it's a game we adore,
Nature's own chuckles leave us wanting more.

But just when we think we've collected enough,
A rogue squirrel chimes in, making it tough.
He snatches a snack and scurries away,
Leaving us laughing, "Oh, what a day!"

Secrets Hidden in the Cradle of Green

In the cradle of green, where shadows entwine,
A riddle of fruits lives, oh what a design!
With leaves as their costume, they peek and they peek,
Whispering secrets, it's quite the cheek!

A samurai squirrel stands guard at the base,
In his tiny brave heart, there's no trace of grace.
With a leap and a bound, he declares "I'm the king!"
While apples giggle and dance in a ring!

A family of deer prances close to the feast,
Sipping sweet nectar, their laughter released.
But one cheeky apple just couldn't resist,
It rolled to the edge; the poor thing was missed!

With a thump and a splash, it landed in soup,
Our cook joined in, declaring a troupe!
As we feast and we toast under the leafy gleam,
Laughter and flavors become our shared dream!

The Resilient Branches

In the garden where shadows play,
A branch danced wildly, come what may.
It wobbled and jiggled, ripe with cheer,
While squirrels all giggled, sipping their beer.

A visitor came, aiming to pluck,
But the branch did a twist, oh what a luck!
It gave one last wiggle, a wink and a grin,
And sent the poor lad tumbling in spin!

"Catch me if you can!" it shrieked with glee,
As cherries fell down like confetti!
The squirrels just laughed, pointing their paws,
At the lad in a fit, aflutter with flaws.

So remember this tale of the branch so spry,
When you're picking fruit on a lazy July.
It just might play tricks, with a jolly old song,
And you'll leave with nothing, but laughter along!

Lush Lullabies

Beneath the boughs where the sweet fruits hum,
A sleepy bee buzzed, all ready to drum.
It sang to the blossoms, soft and slow,
But tripped on its wings, oh what a show!

The flowers all giggled, their petals in sway,
As the bee spun around, in floral ballet.
"Oh dear, dear bee, can you hold your tune?
You're dancing like you've swallowed a spoon!"

The sun peeked down, a smiling old chap,
And joined in the fun, taking off its cap.
Together they swayed, in a silly parade,
Making lullabies that will never fade.

When twilight fell, the laughter remained,
In the garden of dreams, the buzz never waned.
So if you should linger, remember this night,
With a bee that can't sing, but certainly might!

Sighs of the Summer Sun

The sun stretched out, where the laughter lay,
In a hammock of clouds, it chose to stray.
It sighed a hot breath, like a roasted bean,
And asked, "Is it me or is life just a dream?"

Nearby, a squirrel was watching the show,
Nibbling on acorns, moving quite slow.
It snickered aloud, "Oh, the sun's just a fool!
It thinks it can beam, like a kid in a pool!"

The grass rolled its eyes, doing what it could,
While flowers burst out, in giggles, so good.
Nature all chuckled, beneath the bright rays,
As the sun kept on shining, in silly ways.

So if you feel heavy, just look up and grin,
Remember the sun loves a good joke within.
It sparkles and twinkles, in its own funny style,
A warm-hearted guardian, making us smile!

Cradle of Nectar

In a cradle of sweetness, the nectar laid,
A party for bugs, under leaf-shade parade.
They fluttered and spun, intoxicated bliss,
While sipping their drinks, oh, they couldn't miss!

A ladybug shouted, "Dance, my fine friends!
The nectar's delicious, let's see how this ends!"
With wings all a-twirl, they jived on the spot,
But tripped on their wings, oh, what a warm lot!

The ants formed a line, doing two-step prance,
While butterflies joined in a chaotic dance.
The flowers just swayed, in delightful delight,
As petals fell down, like confetti at night.

So if you should wander where delights come alive,
Join the critters in joy, let's see how they thrive.
In nature's grand hall, where laughter is true,
There's always a party, just waiting for you!

The Quiet Giving

In the yard, a tree stands proud,
Whispers soft, never loud.
Its branches sway with glee,
Dropping treasures—oh, wee!

Bees buzz around like they're on a spree,
Chasing flies, just like me.
A fruit falls with a thud,
Rolling past a muddy puddle of mud.

Children run with squeals of delight,
Snatching fruit, a comical sight.
Competition over who can claim,
The juiciest prize in this silly game.

So gather 'round, let's share a laugh,
Nature's bounty, a silly craft.
Under the tree, let's sit and munch,
A feast that feels like a funny brunch.

Nature's Generosity

Beneath the sun, where shadows play,
A quirky tree gives gifts away.
Fruit falls with a squishy sound,
A bouncy surprise upon the ground.

Squirrels chatter, plotting schemes,
For ripe spoils and nutty dreams.
But oh, those apples make them trip,
In their frantic, fruity grip.

A wise old bird, perched high and grand,
Watches as nature's quirkiest band
Juggles fruit, with a splash and a burst,
Who knew a tree could cause such a thirst?

Let's toast to this nature's zing,
With laughter, and the chaos it brings.
A picnic here sounds just divine,
As we munch on flavors so fine.

Portraits of Flavor

Look at those orbs, red and green,
Like little jewels, quite the scene.
They roll and bounce with playful cheer,
Creating laughter far and near.

With every bite, explosion's the game,
Juices run wild, who's to blame?
A dribble here, a splash of juice,
A fruity war—what a wild truce!

What's that clash? A squirrel in flight,
Diving for apples with sheer delight.
A portrait of flavors splashed about,
Around this tree, there's no room for doubt.

So join the fun, wear a bib,
Tasting fruit with giggles, a tasty fib.
Nature's palette is wild and free,
Come take a bite, share with me!

Echoes of Sun-Kissed Days

On sunny days, the laughter rings,
Under the tree, oh, what joy it brings.
Golden fruit, nestled up high,
We wave like crazy, "Oh, just try!"

Each droppin' fruit's an awkward surprise,
Hitting folks like friendly pies.
A giggle here, a squeal over there,
Nature's fun—nothing can compare!

A ladybug winks from leaf to leaf,
As we munch on our fruity grief.
Each bite a giggle, a tickle, a cheer,
Sun-kissed memories so very dear.

So let's dance 'round with blushing cheeks,
In fruity shorts and sunshine streaks.
Under this tree, life is a game,
With laughter echoing, we're never the same.

Harvest of Dreams

In the orchard where laughter grows,
Bobbing apples wearing silly bows.
They giggle as they dangle on high,
Pretending to be the stars in the sky.

The garden gnomes join in the tease,
Telling tales of swift wind and bees.
With each pick, a joke takes flight,
And the fruit becomes our silly delight.

Crisp and round with a wink and a grin,
They tell you secrets, so let the fun begin!
Each bite is a chuckle, sweet and bright,
Our dreams are juicy, our hearts light.

Amid the laughter, the harvest sings,
Of cider spills and mischief it brings.
So gather round, let the silliness spread,
In this orchard, let joy be our bread.

An Invitation to Savor

Grab a basket, the day is grand,
With apples lined in a chaos band.
Each one whispers, 'Pick me today!'
In this funny dance, they all sway.

With a brush of a hand and a teasing spin,
They tumble and roll, let the fun begin!
'Is that a worm?' one shrieks with glee,
'No, it's an apple doing the Macarena, you see?'

We juggle fruits like a circus act,
A few go splat, now that's a fact!
Laughter erupts with each little fall,
Inviting the sun and joy for all.

So come on over, don't delay,
For fruit and fun are here to stay.
With each juicy bite, take a bow,
An apple's elegance in your mouth—wow!

The Dance of Pollinators

Buzzing buddies in a wild ballet,
Flitting around, they love to play.
'Look at us!' shouts the bumblebee,
'We paint the flowers while sipping our tea!'

Dressed in stripes, with a wink and a giggle,
They twirl through petals, just waiting to wriggle.
A ladybug laughs, 'Don't you dare fall!'
As they glide around the apple tree tall.

In a whirlwind of color and delight,
They feast on nectar, what a sight!
Every buzz brings joy and cheer,
In this orchard party, come draw near.

So laugh with the flowers, dance in the breeze,
Join in the fun, if you please!
For harmony reigns where pollinators hop,
In this sweet playground, the laughter won't stop!

Tasting Summer's Embrace

On a sunny day, what a treat!
A picnic spread with fruit to eat.
With a bite of crisp, a giddy squeal,
Summer's embrace is the ultimate deal.

'Is that juice or a fountain of cheer?'
Lemonade laughs, 'I'm the drink of the year!'
Cherries tumble, playing hide and seek,
Leaving bursts of laughter, oh-so-unique.

Open your mouth for the world so bright,
As apples bounce in a golden light.
Each slice a tale of summer's delight,
Where joy and fruit intertwine, just right.

So bring your friends, let the taste buds play,
We'll nibble on joy, and shout hooray!
With every laugh and every bite,
Summer's magic makes everything right.

Shadows of Abundance Under the Sun

Beneath the branches, shadows play,
Chasing each other, hip-hip hooray!
Apples spill laughter, bright and round,
Squirrels dance wildly, joy unbound.

Bugs have a party, buzzing with cheer,
While kids in the orchard hop and steer!
A pie in the making, sweet as can be,
A slice of confusion, oh, what a spree!

Laughter cascades like rain from above,
As fruits throw a bash, they spread the love!
The sun starts to set, a sight to behold,
With all of the antics, a story retold.

Harmonies of Orchard Serendipity

In the orchard where giggles bloom,
Music of bites fills every room!
A squirrel on stage with nuts as his fee,
Belting out tunes, it's pure jubilee!

The apples are winking, bright as a star,
While birds on the branches sing from afar.
A cheeky fox joins the big vaudeville,
With moves that would certainly give you a thrill!

Cider spills laughter, fizzy and sweet,
Dancing in barrels, oh what a treat!
The ants are impressed, they tap their tiny toes,
In a lively fandango, anything goes!

Roots That Reach for the Sky

Roots stretch out wide, a silly sight,
Reaching for clouds, feeling just right!
With bubbles of laughter they tickle the ground,
While teasing the breezes, they whirl all around.

The grass joins the party, swaying with glee,
As worms wiggle tales of wild jubilee.
An underground rave with dirt as the stage,
Organized chaos, what's all the rage?

'We grow down and up!' roots joyfully sing,
Their leafy heads nodding, like they own spring.
While apples up high smugly grin and boast,
'We rule this orchard, let's all raise a toast!'

Whispers of Grateful Harvest

The harvest whispers, secrets in the breeze,
Tickling the apples, shaking the trees.
Grateful giggles burst from the ground,
As critters celebrate all around!

A chicken wears glasses, reading the news,
While tomatoes wear hats, oh, what a ruse!
The cucumbers chuckle, just rolling in mirth,
As pumpkins tell jokes about their own girth!

The joy of the season, a whimsical rhyme,
In this jolly kitchen, it's baking time!
With pies in the oven, oh what a delight,
In laughter we gather, just sharing the bite!

www.ingramcontent.com/pod-product-compliance
Lightning Source LLC
Chambersburg PA
CBHW070314120526
44590CB00017B/2681